NATIONAL
GEOGRAPHIC

The Great Wall
OF CHINA

PIONEER EDITION

By David Jeffery

CONTENTS

An amazing wall stretches across China. It is known as the Great Wall. People call it a "wonder of the world."

Millions of people visit it each year. They come to find out what makes this wall so great.

Yet little is known about the wall. Who built it? When? Why? No one knows for sure.

By David Jeffery

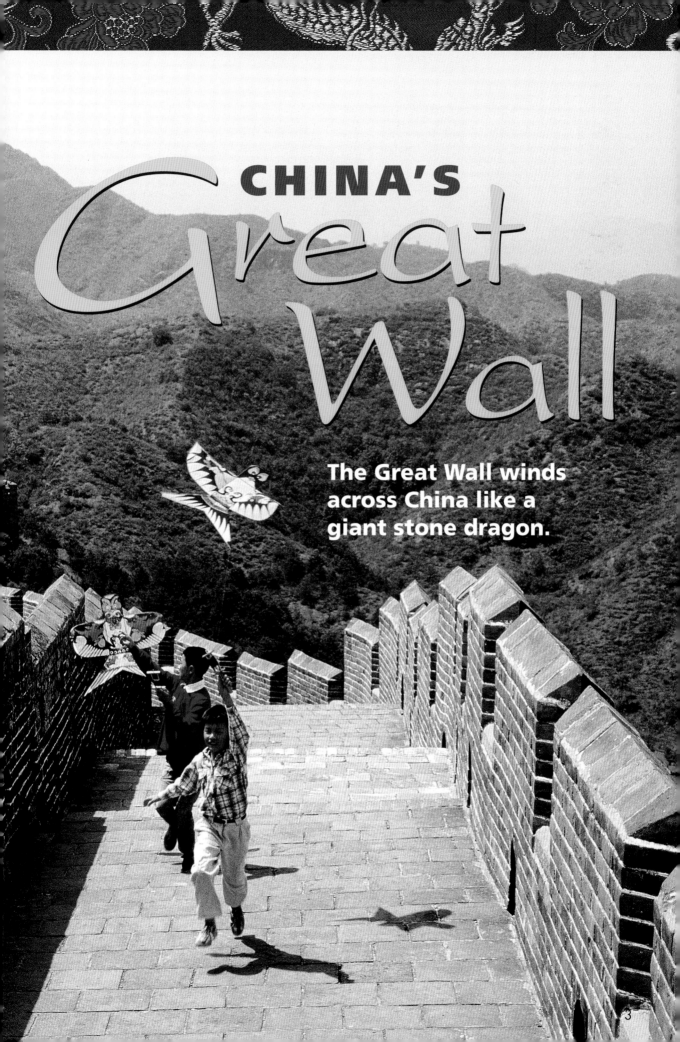

CHINA'S
Great
Wall

The Great Wall winds across China like a giant stone dragon.

ASIA
Great Wall
CHINA

The Emperor's New Wall

In 221 B.C., China got a new leader. His name was Qin Shi Huang Di (chin shur hwong dee). He was China's first **emperor,** or ruler.

He decided to build a long wall. That's the story, anyway. He hoped it would keep the nomads out.

We do not know if the wall was ever built. Perhaps soldiers made a wall of dirt. They did not build the wall we see today.

Not-So-Nice Neighbors

Long ago, China had a problem. It wanted to keep out **nomads,** or wanderers. Nomads lived to the north. They often **raided,** or stole from, the Chinese.

The Chinese tried being tough. They sent armies to attack the nomads. They also tried being nice. They traded with the nomads.

Nothing worked. The nomads kept stealing from Chinese farms and towns.

Friendly Face. *"Dragons" star in Chinese New Year parades. They wind like the Great Wall through city streets. Dragons are signs of good luck in Chinese tradition.*

ALAN WITSCHONKE

Where Is the Wall?

Qin Shi Huang Di died in 210 B.C. No one knows what happened to his wall. It disappeared—if it was ever even built.

More than a thousand years passed. Many **dynasties** rose to power. Those are ruling families.

Then came the Mongols. They were just what China had feared. They were **invaders** from the north. They attacked China in the 1200s.

Wall or no wall, the Mongols won. They ruled for about a hundred years. At last, the Chinese drove them out.

Get the Dirt! *To build China's earliest walls, workers gathered baskets of soil. They dumped soil into wooden frames. Builders then removed the frames. That left a rock–hard wall.*

Old Problems, New Wall

A new emperor took charge. He created the Ming dynasty. That was in 1368. Ming leaders faced the same old problem. They still feared invaders from the north.

What did they do? You guessed it. They built a wall. This time, they made it with bricks and stones. This is the Great Wall that we see today.

Soldiers walked along the wall. They looked for invaders. If they saw danger, they ran to a tower. They built a fire. This warned others about the attack.

5

Wall for Nothing

The wall was long and strong. Even that did not stop attacks in the north.

The Manchu arrived in the 1600s. They refused to leave. In fact, they ruled until 1912. Finally, the Chinese forced them out. China never had an emperor again.

ALAN WITSCHONKE

Built to Last. *The Great Wall is made of brick and stone. Rock and dirt serve as "filling." Baskets and pulleys helped workers ferry materials over steep valleys.*

Old Wall, New Problems

The wall had failed. It had not kept out invaders. Soldiers stopped using it. People started to tear it down. It seemed that no one cared about the wall. Yet visitors loved it.

Over time, the Chinese grew to love it too. Now they are proud of the wall. There is nothing like it in the world.

Today, the Great Wall has many problems. It is very old. Sun and rain beat down on it. Footsteps wear away the rock. The wall is crumbling.

That is why people are working to save the wall. It will take time and money. But the wall is worth it.

The Great Wall once helped protect China. Now China is trying to protect the wall.

Wordwise

dynasty: line of emperors or kings

emperor: ruler

invader: person who takes over another person's land

nomad: someone who moves from place to place, without a regular home

raid: to steal

THE ART ARCHIVE/BRITISH LIBRARY

Emperor Qin Shi Huang Di

Long Story

China's history has many twists and turns. To discover some of them, use your finger to trace a path to FINISH.

START

551 B.C.
Confucius is born. This great thinker influences China for centuries.

221 B.C.
Qin Shi Huang Di unites small kingdoms into one China. He becomes the first emperor.

A.D. 1206
Genghis Khan unites Mongols. These invaders rule all of China by 1279.

A.D. 690
Wu Zhao becomes China's only female emperor.

A.D. 1291
Marco Polo, a famous traveler, leaves China after a 17–year visit. His tales later amaze Europeans.

A.D. 1644
Manchu armies conquer Beijing and set up the Qing dynasty.

A.D. 1912
China's last emperor, Pu Yi, gives up the throne.

FINISH

A.D. 1949
Communists create the People's Republic of China.

A.D. 2001
International Olympic Committee chooses Beijing for the 2008 Summer Games.

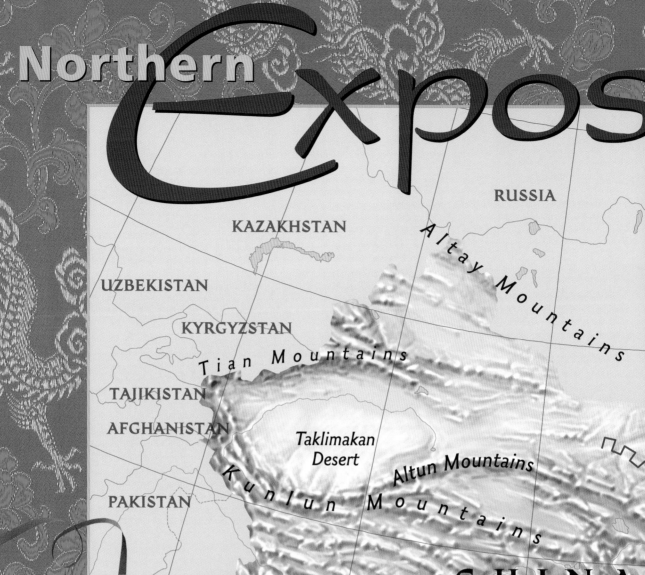

RUSSIA

KAZAKHSTAN

Altay Mountains

UZBEKISTAN

KYRGYZSTAN

Tian Mountains

TAJIKISTAN

Taklimakan
Desert

Altun Mountains

AFGHANISTAN

Kunlun Mountains

PAKISTAN

CHINA

Plateau
of Tibet

Himalaya

NEPAL

BHUTAN

INDIA

BANGLADESH

85°E

95°E

Bay of
Bengal

MYANMAR

LAOS

THAILAND

*C*hina once feared attacks from the north. People built huge walls to keep out invaders. Early walls were made of dirt. Later, a wall was built of stone. Parts of it still stand today. We call it the Great Wall. It is shown in red on the map.

ure

N
W E
S

MONGOLIA

*Mongolian
Plateau*

Gobi Desert

Greater Khingan Range

Manchurian Plain

Mu Us
Desert

Great Wall

⊛ BEIJING

Huang He (Yellow River)

Qin Mountains

Chang Jiang

(Yangtze River)

NORTH
KOREA

SOUTH
KOREA

*Sea of
Japan*

JAPAN

45°N

35°N

*Yellow
Sea*

PACIFIC
OCEAN

*East
China
Sea*

25°N

TROPIC OF CANCER

TAIWAN

15°N

ETNAM

*South
China
Sea*

Hainan

PHILIPPINES

05°E

115°E

125°E

0 ———————— 400 miles
0 ———————— 400 kilometers
Lambert Azimuthal Equal-Area projection

National Geographic Maps

MARK THIESSEN (BACKGROUND)

A Standing
Arm

O. LOUIS MAZZATENTA (CLAY ARMY); DOUG STERN (PAINTED SOLDIER).

Scientists made an amazing discovery in 1974. They uncovered a clay army. They found more than 7,000 soldiers! Each soldier was as big as a real person. Each was made by hand. Each had a different face.

The army was hidden inside a tomb. That is a burial place. It belonged to Qin Shi Huang Di. He ordered workers to make the army. But for thousands of years, no one knew it was there.

Armed and Ready

Scientists have learned a lot from the clay army. It shows how ancient battles may have been fought.

That is because the soldiers stand like a real army. They are in rows. Some soldiers look left. Others look right. The army is ready for an attack.

What is the army guarding? No one knows. That is because parts of the tomb are still buried. What they hold is a mystery.

Guard Duty. TOP: *This clay army guards the tomb of an ancient Chinese emperor.* LEFT: *About 2,000 years ago, each soldier was painted in bright colors. This model shows how the soldiers may have looked long ago.*

Great Wall

Answer these questions to find out what you have learned.

1 Why did the Chinese build the Great Wall?

2 Who were the Mongols?

3 Why is China proud of the Great Wall?

4 What is the wall like today?

5 What can we learn from the clay army found in 1974?